DATE DUE

KAMIKAZE
GODS
& SUICIDE MULES

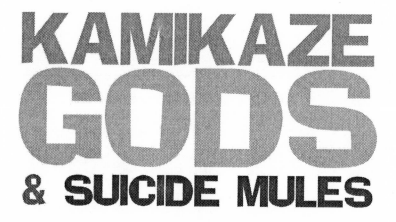

the Reno Four

iUniverse, Inc.
New York Lincoln Shanghai

Kamikaze Gods and Suicide Mules

iUniverse, Inc.

For information address:
iUniverse
2021 Pine Lake Road, Suite 100
Lincoln, NE 68512
www.iuniverse.com

Special thanks to Ed Galm for cover design.

To contact any member of The Reno Four write to 11565 Old Virginia Road, Reno, Nevada 89521.

ISBN: 0-595-28906-1 (Pbk)
ISBN: 0-595-65933-0 (Cloth)

Printed in the United States of America

Contents

Contents

Contents

Introduction

One found a laundry room flier that left his death wish for obscurity unfulfilled. Two sought some poetic distance from his poetic existence. Three poured his heart into his family, and then himself. Four lit a fire and spread it so that everyone imagined they could walk through it.

The Reno Four (Scott Shulim, Scott Elliott, R.G. Saderup and Anthony Ziegler) initially met in a Silver State Fiction Writers group, in a strip mall community center room in Reno, Nevada. They exchanged wary glances, sized each other up, and said, "Hey." The rest, as they say, is pretty uneventful.

They met some more, in casino keno coffee shops and ghost town high school libraries and open mics and closed bookstores, and they talked and thought about everything and nothing including writing a book, but didn't.

Over 10 years later, they didn't give a crap and did something about it.

Here is the sum of their parts, and perhaps a little more.

Days With No Name

by R. G. Saderup

Days With No Name

I.

This moment will already be gone, a piece of impotent dust settling into obscurity, and there will be nothing said, nothing noted, nothing described.

It will be nothing that fades into nothing.

The thought is both amusing and frightening. When it comes down to the most intimate detail of life, it might be a complete failure.

Vanished and forgotten.

Hard to laugh about it, hard not to cry about it, hard to sit here and not want to do something to divert it, but it is useless, because some moments in life are empty, inconsequential, and better left to drain away.

And it's already gone. A new moment has arrived and it seems as big and unrelenting as the previous. Both spin into whatever conclusion they will become.

What to make of it?

I look down at my stomach, wipe away a spot of spaghetti sauce, left of the navel, look out the door. A pair of Magpies fly into the yard, hop on the cars, and find nothing of interest…It is a warm evening. Spring has finally arrived. Rob's dog is barking. My cat cleans its paws, looks outside, also.

My other neighbor just arrived home, goes inside her apartment.

Lee is her name. She fucked Rob, my other neighbor. I saw them on her porch couch, grabbing each other, bathrobes open, as I pulled into the drive they broke apart, then they fled to the inside of her apartment. I laughed to myself.

Never did expect to end up like this, lonely on the outskirts of Reno watching my neighbors, finding amusement here. I probably had it coming, I have met a lot of people, but I didn't let them mean much. Most of them are gone now. There are still a few friends hanging on, but the majority surrendered to their lives and moved on, doing what they had to do.

I arrived here through the demands of a dream…something from childhood. To find myself, I suppose, or some self sought conclusion. In a small town, without having something to hope for, you just die there, and for a long time all I could think of was getting away from that little place; escaping however I could. Now, I look back, and I wonder how wrong I might have been, that maybe I saw things the way I wanted to see them, and my perspective was all mixed up. Now it seems like that town was the only real home I ever had. Funny how the mind can do that, trip you, put the resentment inside—rotting and festering, building into a good sorrow, a good ulcer. Not that I didn't have my fun along the way, but it seems more childish than anything else does. Never could grow up. What was that line from Kay's song...? 'Boy-child in a man's body'.

I never liked that song. She was most likely right, the way she always seemed to be. That's why I couldn't be with her anymore. Always feeling wrong and guilty. I couldn't walk around that way any longer, too confusing, too twisted. My identity felt buried. So I came here and hid it externally. A man has to feel his pride, or otherwise he just dumps himself in a gutter and stays there. Plenty have.

We still talk, Kay and I, as friends, but even now with it behind us, I can still taste it on the back of my tongue, like some chemical that sours my mouth. At that point, I get away from her. Rage is an even worse killer.

"You're finally doing it," she said the other day, "cutting everyone away from yourself, living in isolation."

Yeah...maybe?

Or maybe I'm tired of the con-artists, the thugs, the assholes, the multitude of Jones's, the car salesmen...everything that makes life so damn degrading.

It's like this lesbian said at a party I went to, "Everybody is sooo 'fucked up'..."

Last night stars
fell,
one by one.

It was glorious,
a sensation. They arced dramatically through a black sky.
They burned into nothing,
disappearing in the density of the universe,
forever a mystery.

3

II.

Spider
black spot on a white ceiling
moves slowly with an uncertain path.

Watching this,
maybe for too long,

thinking: a spider never wants
for food,

just wanders,
builds its web when needed,

lives within providence.

Recognize the fact
that the world
is without reason
thriving in unending chaos.
Absurdity exists
because society
tries to make amends
through shame
through righteousness.
Only in the absurd
where all things have no scheme
is a man free.

In the crawl of spiders
in the flight of a magpie,
in the bark of a dog…who
ask for nothing,
I find reassurance.

III.

This was once a dude ranch,
then a whore house,
on the skirts of Reno.
A little white-haired lady
bought it and raised her kids here.

Her daughter, turning white-haired
herself, raised her own children on these
five acres,
collects the rent,
feeds the birds, the raccoons, the skunks.

Stray cats wander in and out.
Red-tail hawks fly in the blue skies.
Screech owls blow up against windows
during midnight storms.
There are untold stories buried here,

and a half dozen pets in the backfield.

On one side
Lee rattles the walls,
hammers things into place.
At midnight she takes a shower,
the pipes shake and groan
beneath floorboards and trampled carpets.

On the other, Rob's dog
barks at rocks.
The Irish Setter pisses if you pet him,
bites your fingers.
His master puts fishing gear

into a new boat and on the weekend
takes it to the mountains,
returns with whole salmons,
big fish. Some, five or six feet long.
Sometimes my two neighbors wander back and forth
to each other with blue drinks in their hands.
Laugh and talk. I try to ignore their conversations.

There is a modern artist in the little house
out back.
But he is too bitten and scarred
by life to talk with
anymore.

This was once a dude ranch,
then a whore house.
A sealed door connects each apartment.

I live between their oddities,
their kindness.

IV.

The morning creeps to the edge of a branch
awakens in the ocean of the universe.

This piece of Earth
that feeds me,
is changed overnight
by the weather.
A natural course of things…
the spider that moves to a corner
and builds its nest.
I am
that close to the world at large,
nothing but
a shaft of weathered light
between it and I.

My words,
the day,
become ash.

V.

Hundred-year-old cottonwood trees
stand in clusters of dry leaves
strangled in a mottled ground.
Blackbirds shadow the splayed branches,
a tempest sky prevails. Granite mountains
loom brown and gray.

The morning transcends the earth
grafts the edges of the valley floor.
I notice it like I would
the arrival of a stranger.

These old houses
among fading grass
sink into wet ground.
Leaves build into mounds
cling to the foundations.

Dry roof shingles pop
leap with dark wings
to crash into the winter shadows.
Chimes ring,
heralding the storm front
winds,
chatter like anxious birds.
The long grass weaves into gray.
With each gusting wind
these walls resist.

A stretch of clouds
along mountaintops
clouds the size of mountains rolling

to graze the valley floor.
A dark shadow stretching.
branches tremble,
the ground stands still.
A hundred thousand drops
descend in a single wave.
A rampant drumming begins against wood
rocks,
hammering on metal...
RAIN!
Child of oceans.

RAIN!
Ghostly dancer.
Cutting stone.
Eroding wood.
Rotting metal.
Silencing birds.

RAIN!

Black fire
This day.
Ting, tong, drubble, drubble.

tap, tap, tap.

RAIN!

Slung among roots, hollows
against wall and window
forming in black ponds
and shimmering currents
breaking ground.

RAIN!

Cold air
and RAIN
slip through cracks
in windows and doors.
I stuff paper napkins
into the fissures,
which work, 'til they get soaked.
The rivulets run
horizontal across window panes.

VI.

People
I know
have their lives
in good order.
Sunday church and then the park.
Monday laundry, class on Tuesday
Wednesday for families.
Thursday for friends.

Friday out.
Saturday shopping.
A revolution of carefully
constructed time,

and myself
I live in absurdity,
drifts of action,
spontaneous decisions.
Dirty dishes in the sink,
paintings stacked every which way
against walls,
socks on the floor.
Unfinished projects.

A dresser drawer
hangs open.
Above it, on the top
a clock winds
through the seconds.
Next to that
a silent night lamp,
yellowed shade a shadow

on a plain white wall
which has thin fingers of light stretching

from a window
across the texture.
I am amazed at the color
of white
socks on my feet,
resting them on an unmade bed
in the middle of the morning
with rain outside.

I cull coins from
a coffee can,
tangible little stones that I throw away,
enough for breakfast
and a load of laundry.

Clothes,
a week's worth
pushing towards the walls
falling coil upon coil
stained by coffee,
sweat, spaghetti sauce
spreading across the floor.

I gather them into one mass.
An uncertain dread weeds

itself around me
immobilizes me.
The gas company shut the heat off,
the bank sent me notice that I am six dollars
fifty-seven cents overdrawn.

No work.
One bald tire, ready to explode,
worn brakes.

I am what I am...

A faucet drips
and my cat keeps staring at me
as if I have forgotten something.
Oh yes,
the ex-wife moved to California
with my daughters.

The elastic band
on a sock has snapped
leaving it with a yawing mouth.
There is also a hole in the toe.
I wear it anyway.
No one can see your socks.

I shake out the rugs

sweep

watch a spider
caught by the flick of the broom
curl into a black ball
on the linoleum
dying on the cold floor
a tiny irreversible scar
in time and space,
my own constant realization
that I am a figment
in the course of the universal sensation.

VII.

I talk to my cat
and
he listens gracefully
with great distractions
in mind:
a spider on the floor,
dead fly in the window.
Nothing is like
it was in the beginning
when first awakenings
and the first minute blazed into the eyes.
Little toes, little fingers
pushing aside carefully erected barriers
turned the Earth upon itself
to hold together the pebbles and leaves…

suckling
rain, the earth, the cloth
mining the whistle of sound.
Above, the sky billowing
into feeling

and the trees were giants standing against the storm.
It was an awkward
motion of swimming
from the hollow
of new shoes and unfamiliar skin
into open air.

VIII.

To sing a song
to yourself
even though the notes are
winter flies trying to escape through
a window screen
is daylight for a dark mood.
Before losing the words
Because memory
Is slow and dull
and slighted
there is that morning air in the lungs
a solitary feeling
of the singer
holding that high note,
oblivious to everything.

In a _LaunderLand_
the conversation takes place
on a big screen t.v.
The abnormalities of society
are slowly dissected and exploited
by a head-shaking talk show host.
A bored audience looks on.
Washers hum,
vibrate,
dryers clunk

jeans, and shirts revolve.
Outside, magpies, blue jays, and sparrows
stalk the parking lot

carry tidbits to their young.

I wait like everyone else
for clothes to dry
for time to move on,
for the storm to stop
for someone with courage
to turn that damn television off.

Jesus!

IX.

I wander the same streets
the same avenues
looking for something different
and find yesterday
the day before
and tomorrow.

To asphalt to dirt
my mind stricken
in a disjointed walk
fast then slow
an irresistible impatience
irrational and remarkable
hides me.

I've been everywhere man...
Johnny Cash followed the burning
sands.
He probably felt

little orbs of raindrops
catch the light
then disintegrate into concrete.

I figure if I could sing like Johnny Cash
I'd probably think of Reno
as a little city
with casinos and rain on its
gray streets,
but to me
Reno is everywhere man,
and rain is unusual.

X.

In a casino coffee shop
I notice

she has good legs
beginning at the edge of
tan shorts that are part of her uniform
ending in white gym shoes,
the kind a nurse would wear.
Her face is matronly.
She fills my cup
takes my order.
The sun angles
across cars in the parking lot.
It bursts into a bright leaf,
punches through windowpanes.

I eat my eggs, toast, hash browns
bacon.
Smoke a cigarette.
She asks,
"Is everything okay?"

I sit here.
Fearing what?
I can't name it.
I gaze at the
ceiling,
then level eyes
on the wall, the parking lot,
the waitress,
the day.

I say
take it by its throat
this animal,
console it
placate it.
Then throttle it.

Young women in a café
dressed to serve
the icon of social providence.
Business suits and credit cards
flash like smiles.
Hair is done
in shining lamplight.
Clothes are fit to absorb
the occasional glance.

They make their money
go home.
The candles on the tables
Burn.
A new order of toast browns,
The day posts its keno numbers.

XI.

I open my mouth
and gulp air.
I swallow the dead.

My grandfather,
my grandmother
my mother;
the Kennedys,
Van Gogh,
Henry Miller,
even Richard Nixon
swoop down into my belly
then sit there in lumps
of slowly dissipating matter
becoming aches in my kidneys
liver, spleen, intestines,
and bladder.
Most of all, they
burst free as conversations.

XII.

Listening to hazy
rock-n-roll
on a cheap plastic radio-
cottonwood seeds filling the air
falling like snowflakes.
It's a hundred degrees.
Mosquitoes are out early
biting, drawing blood.
The sun weakens
slowly,
slowly
losing to the evening sky
to the gravity of eastern mountains.
to three beers and a bottle of schnapps
that brings the lazy walk of neighbors
talking of Kona buds,
and trout
planted yesterday
in city streams.

XIII.

Haven't felt
The dawn so sleeping,
Unperturbed
Magical
Like a child's face

Even birds brilliantly silent
From the ground, wakened
Standing upright
Shadows
Flying
Wonderful morning.

XIV.

In the reckless
winds
there come the sounds of mountains
being shaped.

Sand moves in the air
the desert flowers
rock becomes ash.

XV.

Even the walls sweat in this place,
trickles of perspiration
a nuisance like gnats
down my neck.
WISHING to scream
at my ex-wife
my girlfriend,
the lawyer
maybe my neighbors,

give me a suitcase
a gun, a song...
A cold drink of water.

XVI.

She holds me

There is an imprint
of a watch, white in the tanned skin
of her wrist.

All night
the prayers were in secret,
each other.

XVII.

A sing-song movement through life
into labyrinths
of back alley's,
always a mysterious doorway.

XVIII.

In unexpected places

A wandering dance
along fence posts
to the mouths of canyons
where it seems the things
farthest away are the most obvious.

A feeling of swimming
in the velvet
of an ocean
current
weighed against arms.

A walk over grit

in the dark
here the moonlight
there a landscape.

Always the feeling
of balance
in the stretch of fingers.

XIX.

A thin end of day
a weary peace,
waters of night.
Swollen feet
motionless
weightless
free,
a breeze wraps itself
around the skin
bathing flesh.

XX.

The empty drone of the refrigerator
Fills the afternoon silence.
Five times
I have got up from the couch
Went to look for something
Opened and closed the door.

What do I want?

There are those times
When wandering back and forth
Looking in refrigerators
Cupboards
And out of windows
Is all I can do,

Maybe sometimes
There is nothing more important
Than sitting
And watching the table fan

Swivel right to left
Left to right.

XXI.

The wind blew all day
Tearing down old branches,
Pecked the windows with splinters of rain.

I wanted soup for a sore throat
Found a cup of yogurt instead.
Tried to stay in bed.
Went to the store
Twice,
The second time with money.

I wonder if she heard anything I said,
and I listened to the sound of wet grass.

Philosophy and soup taste the same.

XXII.

Out past the trees hackle
Out past the slow turn of a hawk's wing
Above a field
And out past the rooftops
In the dusty noon light
Thunderclouds above the mountains
Wet the ground with shadows.

XXIII.

Tangled winter tree limbs
shoots of green showing
In black bark.

That feeling again

A new light in doorways and windows,
Skin flaking off
Dry leaves crushing into dust.

Again
The feeling.
forget this weary smile
And laugh out loud.

Through the door, the dark shadow of night, it is the sound of snakes hissing in the quiet branches. I sit like Rodin's thinker staring at the stars, the sky, and my neck begins to ache under the weight of thought. A hopeless dreamer, I, stuck in the mud of a restless society.

A crimp in my neck begins to strangle me and jerk my head back to the horizon, dizzy, and the nearest objects, cottonwoods with leaves as black faeries.

I steady myself.

From the whispers in the branches the words: sky, air, ground, water.

You

You

You

Who are you

I see myself as a boy, thin and freckle-faced, dust and sun roughening skin. I jog after my big brothers and their friends, trying to match their longer strides.

"Hurry," they say, but my feet aren't fast enough, and it agitates them as I catch up and then fall back again.

"Too slow," they scoff and scowl.

A thin freckle-faced boy, short of breath, strangled my intimidation.

The cottonwoods are now swimming with an evening wind, the branches creek. A narrow limb falls to the ground, disappearing in the dark grass. I walk out to the street. It is a quiet street, very little traffic. Once in a while a car will blow by and be gone. There are ranches, cattle. and scattered houses.

I rent from a small pot-bellied lady with a cigarette clenched between fingers. She worries about the skunks and raccoons, the hawks and owls, the groundhogs and squirrels. Where will they go, now that they routed an interstate through these meadows?

Progress...

Go to the desert
Speak your name,
Leave it.

The wobbly, the mick
The Redman, the Chinaman, spooks and wopps,
Grunts, hobos, golddiggers.
Grease monkeys, roughneckers, goat ropers.
Roots.
Ground
Skies and mountains,
An American garden.

I Wear the World's Clothes

I wear the world's clothes
a hand-me-down
nostalgia of roses
and pallid skies.

My own ornaments
loose shoes
tattered socks
footprints left
behind.

A ludicrous sanity
myself,
earth and water
vanity and pride.

At my feet
dead-ends of pathways-
beloved grass, diamonds and
inheritance.

Deliberate, fashionable,

miraculous

ages
with
sorrow,
jasmine,
musk;
sun and belief.

Downtown

Eye on an evening.
Saved a couple of bucks
on some cigarettes,
two for ones'
the store clerk
had hidden under the counter.

Went downtown to
a poetry reading,
crowded with hip-hop kids
shouting about things

so I bought an expensive beer
with the extra money from the smokes,
even threw a quarter
in the tip jar
went

and sat in a chair outside,
watched the pedestrians walk casually by:
in and out of the street light
even gave a
couple of cigs to a down and out
tried talking to him, but he just walked on-
even bums don't give a damn much nowadays-
so I watched him fade
into the timeless cracks
of this all too often lonely city.

My God

What a day
back and forth across
asphalt
of a country club's parking lot
sore feet,
burnt eyes,
sweat,
bodily trying to get a job done
and when no one is looking,
amidst hauling ladders, paint buckets and
listening to the taunts
of a delusional foreman,
I make do with a moment
to look at something,
like a mountain
in a blue sky
or think about what the buffalo crossing endless plains
must have looked like a long time ago.

It isn't simple to live
these days
even imagination can turn
the day into a storm,
and it's always the same talk
the same innuendo
the same foreman
and it isn't right not to say something-
stand your ground,
show them what kind of man you are...
so, it's a hard look in the eye

that goes round and round
all day with no end in sight.

Maybe it is just too many days
like this
wishing to be on that mountain
watching those buffalo,
wishing that asshole would get stomped
into the ground with those restless hoofs.

Like a cat wanting outside
I pace
across the same floor
thinking about things that nobody
wants to think about.

Why bother
with how long that sun
has been in the sky,
or how old a stone is
and if they move about
(ever kept a garden?)
or why the mind leaves childhood,
or if you believe enough
you might just be able to breathe under water,

maybe it isn't worth the trouble

but

the same song
is different to the individual ear
the way some colors make
others laugh.

Among Happenstance

Chairs
tables
knick-knacks
the hemp shirts
antiques
paint peeling
a strange woman's curious world
where things
in a showcase
along a little street
by a river
in a moment of silence
a customer
coming through the door
and while alone
to look through what is obvious
trying to learn more
whatever secrets there are
eyes telling of a laugh
makes me forget
the question I had wanted to ask.

"Want to meet"

I say, then
go about my business
thinking all those
specific thoughts that are
too numerous
to keep
and float around my head
like a thousand birds
in a perfect blue sky

then I stop
wondering
what it is I like about you
beyond the bodily attraction
or the excitement
of a woman standing nearby

must be the laugh
and the voice
and those all too mysterious eyes.

Can't quite say
with this tongue
the meaning of it
so I wait
moments away
from what I believe should be
a reply.

Today

I was miserable
joyless
alone
a stranger

until I saw a middle aged
couple
on vacation
and they were laughing.

I guess
that life is meant to be that way
turbulence
then a moment where it stands still
before moving on.

A Mile Beneath the Night

by Scott William Elliott

Something in the Night

Watering the lawn
10 pm
yellow stars slink across sky
Something in the night is watching me
and watching you
It is some beast in the alley,
a creature in a tree,
some subterranean up for air
or maybe it is you
and I am the beast moving
the sprinkler

Something in the night is watching me
and it will not move,
will not come forth,
will not kill-
stalking me only with eyes
hearing my breathing,
my heartbeat,
my footfall
on the un-mowed grass
It is near
and you are distant
or dead or a flickering dream

Something in the night is watching me
knocking at my soul,
whispering through my blood,
muttering at my heart
I am the pillar of salt
and it is the laughing bird

on a limb
or the warm breath at my bare feet
It will not let me be
but it will not seize me
It simply exists
as I exist
standing in my backyard, fenced in,
yellow stars slinking by
Something in the night is watching me
Watering the lawn
10 pm-

Agony With A View

No one speaks
and no one smiles
In this room
you and I
face to face
with the entire night
between us
We wait
We wait
for something to break
for something that can touch us
for something real
more real than ourselves-
the roof to cave in, gunshots,
sirens, laughter-
Existing is so difficult
and on a moon swept wall
our shadows touch
unaware

TS

Broken off
Leaf-like, fluttering
down a ghostly center
as the great body
saunters along getting away
up and down days and nights
as a mirage of wary faces
tinkers with fragile dreams
delicately removing heart
meticulously fumbling with spirit
Spirit man
Broken
at the bottom
on rocks, on words, on morality
All the blood washes away
Here in a wasteland of limb and hindsight
we count time itself-
we judge the machinery of solar systems
we name each movement
We pass on
our tainted segments
of eternity-

Boneyard, You

Only the sea is real
Nothing else lasts or matters
And what of all the words,
what of all the glory
and dreams scotch-taped
to a page of scribbled lines-
Where is there space for all that?
What is in the boneyard, when,
At last, the waves come?
You cling to your spiritual machinery
but the mechanical operation of faith
has rusted
the blood hardens
the eyes fixed
then you know
only the sea is real…
and the bird above flying
so high-

A Mile Beneath the Night

Can you hear that?
Love doesn't flower
all too spectacular
Even with great distance
the bloom is lavender
and fragile
Reunions wilt away
Like the lilly dropped
In the driveway in August
And sleep is the blackest rose of all
Do you hear the sound?
Something far beneath us toils
lower than spirit can
take us
I curl in a cocoon midst a thousand miles
of desert sage
You're off to California
In a white car at midnight
And the digging never ends
The night expands with you
as my walls close in
I dream of wind and music
and throw flowers at shadows
as you arrive somewhere
far away
Can you hear it?
Far below us...
a mile beneath the night
the digging
the tunneling
continues on

Kamikaze Gods and Suicide Mules

Like stars
Like seasons
Like disease
It's working on impulse
Two souls
trying to find each other-

The Silent Moment

The silent moment comes only
when you can't take it-
not when you need it,
crave it, pray for it.
The wheel does not let up
and when at last the timeless moment
finds you
it has turned against you
because fear has got you first
because guilt has got you first
because spite has got you first
and the moment takes you for a ride-
The kids won't come home or
your lover will not call or
a dream has just folded like
a cracker box in the trash or
there is nothing, nothing, nothing!

It is not a thing of liberation;
You are condemned to that moment.
It is the very end of something.
It is the very beginning of something
As you sit strangled against your mind-

All your anguish
All your soul
All your waiting

Your silent moment will come

Moonlit Hills

Now only the fixed stare
of animal eyes
Beasts shining
in nocturnal comfort
under stars without names
in forests without owners
from lives without time
feasting, feasting
Feasting on you, feasting on me
Slipping back into black voids
through scarcely moonlit hills
they carry something of mine away

Glue

I got mind
I got body
I got spirit
I got the American childhood
and the government on my back
Got the bills in the mail
and a job in the warehouse
but it won't stay all together

I got mind
I got body
I got spirit
I got small town parades
and smiles at the post office
I have winter walks in the park
but it's all come loose
I have the faint feel for the dream
and some vision left too
I have the black hollow embrace of night
and I walk like a King from room to room
but I can't keep it all together
so I'll search every horizon
grace my nights with remembrance
and watch the school buses pass
Take my daughter to piano
Throw the ball with my son
I have a little more patience
than I used to have
Got a halfway steady hand
but it's coming apart

I got mind
I got body
I got spirit
I got a great house
on the acropolis
crumbling down

Warehouse

Underfoot the American dream
Caged, yet holding on
like lovers clutching keepsakes
After hanging by a blue collar
for 20 years
you're basically just pissed off
shuffling idle moments with retrospect
No more cold beer
and warm women at sunset
No more safe embrace and a wild crawl
to a haven called home
Only cracked callused hands
and a new age limp into retreat
to contemplate ceiling paint
and wonder about TV dinners
Pop the pain pills
till it all bleeds away
in the black phantasm of night

and the nights go by
and the days go by
Summer, Autumn,
Winter
Occasionally still laughter
from the shower
or a faint reflection
of spirit
and there are days that you remember the dream
and days you don't
and so many days that it simply

doesn't matter
because most days
aren't remembered at all

(Untitled)

Stepping stone
Silver light
A green surface
A face
unchanged in moonlight
Breath slight and unnoticed
Gentle filling
of secret places
in eddies, in caves, in tree roots
Deep
Noonday sun shafts
of memory
fade like footfalls
of those before us

I see the river
winding secretly
Time tells not
depth or shadows
Only reflection
silver and green
The dilemma is present
Worship the past
Worship the past
never see
never hear
a thousand places
the waters seep

Unfinished

Like candle wax
melted down porcelain
on the nightstand
amidst lamp, phone, alarm clock
The Madonna
Jesus in her arms
not deformed but
strangely incomplete
blank faces barely
distinguishable, uncommon
in a common tangle
but still it is waiting
only waiting
sincere in lamplight
haunting in moonlight
like the sculptor
the poet
the beasts and saints
of history and today
like you
like me
unfinished

Maybe it's the Light

I am in fear of you
maybe because you know me
and I don't
Maybe because fruit grows
from your limbs of intention
and I would be content
to winter in the warmth
of your shadow
to sleep there
to weep there

I am in fear of you
maybe because you reach for me
and I don't
Maybe because truth, like a clown,
dances on your every word
and I would be grateful
to find a way in
to bear cluttered dreams
on that sunny field
and I could smile
uninhibited
as I burn away
so slowly

I am in fear of you
maybe because you follow me
maybe because you'll come too close
and I'll snuff out
that most beautiful spark
and we'll suffer wholly

a black autumn love
forever turning without
anything to hide from
to run to
to die with

These Nights Become Many

It goes beyond poetry
Goes beyond reflection
and hope
It comes down to hatred
and a fragile shell
of broken sleep
Late night hours spent sitting
in darkness
no longer waiting for light
There is no process
No chronological reference
No resolution
Only absolution and isolation
or seasoned rage
to fill empty hands
Fuck poetry
Language is meaningless
There is desperation and there is belief
and belief is the greatest gamble of all

LA December

Crashing through
a slight strand of palm trees
the sun envelops
pink roses
beautiful and artificial
again and again
day after day
tailor painted and unfolded
for the perfection
of our enchantment

Even the Pretty Girls Had Eyes

Under pale skies
desperate for danger
I went soul shopping
and the streets were graced
with white lace
and the buildings shone
of the Bronze Age
and even the pretty girls had eyes
of metallic taste
The sewers backed up
with silver
and the cars all melted away
An old man perished right there
in the winter of his mind
So I window shopped
compared prices
had a beer
paced around
And evening came
like a stone from the sky
all bright figures lurked away
and the moon did rise
bloody but peaceful
and you know,
I went home again,
empty handed-

Moonlit Hills 2

In the desert
in the tainted glass night
where the sage glows dimly
under partial moon
the shiny eyes open
of something stalking the vastness
inside
but nothing changes, the stars
burn out one by one
hair falls out
memory forgets
day does dawn once again
dimming the shiny eyes
of the aging nocturnal dream

Flowers

Some feelings grow awkward
like flowers from cracks
in concrete
or voices crowded
with desolation, faces
ill-lit by a spark
that nearly revealed an answer
with a glimmer of truth in
the eyes

then darkness again
the desolate voices again
and flowers in cracks
that nobody saw
to begin with-

Traffic

I said good-bye to them in a parking lot
kissed their young faces in fading light;
the summer muted and still.

Then at a red light
they were behind me
waving furiously like a crowd
in an old war film
with the ships coming in.

Green light—they followed
waving still in the stretching parallax
but still
the look in their eyes was bright.

Straining through rear view
they made the turn off.
A headlight, a blur of grill-
my children, my children
flashing in metallic images-
a most terrible distance
as they headed out
fading into traffic.

Non-real Poem

It all passes
and what in the end
will be left that's real?
Hollow footsteps on creaky floors?
Strangled light from a questionable sun?
I'm telling you-
It's not easy being non-real.
Look at the moon
the stars
the ribbon of desire
from my door to yours.

The only thing I ever wanted
To be non-real
was all this space
between us.

Gym Class

Upstairs
caged in a corner
battle-wrecked and leaning
on a splintered crutch of youth
I scan the bodies below:
Bending, soaring, suspended
on ropes or bars-
My daughter on a trampoline,
my son on the rings.
Suddenly I'm broken,
my eyes bleed
and memory pushes the blood
to a place where I was a boy
bending and soaring too
before manhood
before baldness
before beer
before America-
the youth now passed to my children
and the boy I was
stolen away, murdered, buried,
rotted in a childhood coffin
before anger
before hatred
before being chased
into the wasteland,
before graduations
and visions that were formless-

My children look up, sneak a wave
I smile back

though I'm dislocated,
crushed at the spine
as a cold shadow consumes me
I sink into a small chair

I watch from my shell
all the vitality and achievement
like a dreamer in the park
admiring all that slips away.

The Crystal Line

When the words run dry
and my world and yours
revolve separately
When the death of the light in your eyes
is not enough to cloud the skies
When I find you stooped over
your nerves reading dirges
in a stranger's doorway

I will take from you
something that is left

I will sow a life from the
worn skin of your soul
I will carve a picture of a brighter day
from your broken spirit
I will exhume humble deeds
I will sail a sea from your tear
I will hold you in the half-light
of an eclipsed dream
and I will be
    and I will be

Carnival

I entered a carnival passing through town
and shared my past with
screaming teenagers and exhibitionists.
Squeezing through generation gaps
I walked my childless twilight,
closed my eyes to dazzling scintillation
and shuffled blindly in a sedated frenzy
past twisted lines for rides,
past boundless dollar bills at concession stands,
past sweethearts strolling arcades hand in hand.
The smell was sweat and perfume,
soda and cotton candy.
The future was sticky promises in the red
and yellow striped corners, where with
bottles propped and prizes stocked
I held the world in my hand.

I've lived a thousand boyhoods,
a thousand realizations.
I looked into all the faces,
all the lights,
the endless stars.
There were so many things I was going to be.

.549.5

If it had been me or you
there would have been no need
for the ER room.
He stood there Christ-like
ripped from an American crucifix,
matted hair and beard, puss and blood,
urinating in his holy Levi's,
and the nurses hollered and the doctors
complained and the security guard
tucked in his shirt
and the daisy-eyed lab girl said:
"Look, .549.5 alcohol level, and he's still alive!"
It was time for shift change
And we stood and pointed
like Roman judges until he silently went
to a small bed
pulling a blanket over his head, his own
sacred cave.
We went home for the weekend, came back, and
no one has seen him since.

Halloween

I will never be one of them-
people of such order
and blank acceptance
Took my kids to the good neighborhood
for Halloween,
walking smooth sidewalks bordering
flats of mowed lawns and manicured hedges
before white collar homes
with double wooden doors
and two car garages

I will never be one of them-
an ordinary American
in the current of the mainstream
I walk a different path struggle with
surroundings on the inside
They struggle with stock options
and tax-exempt charitable contributions

I will never be one of them-
I watch my kids run door to door
Content men and women drop
candy in the bags
The moon is high over this
Green suburban neighborhood
A single grid in the dreamscape
of America

I will never be one of them
But I'll have hope
my kids will be

Lost In

Did you know that I knew
what I had become
lost to words
lost to dreams
turned awkward in your brown iris soul
where God staggered behind
some cheap statue.
I destroyed so much of you
Crushed you like a champagne glass
Threw your animals out windows
Burned your ranch style home
Murdered your interior decorator
Fucked your Mexican maid
Damned your dusty churches.

Did you know that I knew
What you had become?
Even before I smashed it all
and used the debris
to seal me away in a room
alone with your deserted things
(the old silenced dreams)
that I often rummage through
and cradle in my broken hands.

The Moon Crosses Your Soul

There have been too many
stretches of awkward hours dragged through
the frostbitten yearning of a winter
embrace
Too many lopsided nights
in my small bed
with the wind at my back
Too many times thinking of all that you were
while I held myself
deflated and foolish
whirling leaf-like in the crystal, emerald
and crimson chokehold
of your spirit
How is it the mountain crown
whispers your name?
Tell me how the moon
crosses your soul

When I'm safe in my dim chamber
of self
I want the danger of you

Neon bleeds into Reno dusk
Your green hills far away
and there is light in these eyes
from the warmth I remember
But this is no song of joy

With the night come dreams
Sometimes you're laughing
sometimes crying

I see the light in your window
a tear
on a pensive face
I reach for you…

I see the moon shining
off the snow
of the distant mountain

Beggar, Priest, Murderer

Floyd held his 12-gauge like a golden lamp
as he pushed open my door,
"Jesus man, get up, they're here!"
I stumbled in my underwear outside
and saw the countless silhouettes coming in
from the moonlight.
"Oh," I mumbled, "what the hell…"
I went back in and stared at the wall to make sure
it was the same wall I had stared at the night before.
I heard a gunshot.
I was loading my 30/30 when Floyd
busted in again.
"Jesus man, hurry your young dumb ass up!"
We got out into the middle of the driveway
and leveled our guns to the onslaught of shadows
wielding clubs, stones, and knives.
We took the safetys off and trembled, stole
a quick glance at one another.
"I once wanted to be a preacher," he said,
"but right now I'd rather beg."
Then we looked back through our gunsights knowing
we would be terrible murderers
before the sun rose.
And we squeezed our triggers and pondered
which world was truly ours.

Grounded

Nothing left now
but a dusty lamp shade
and my shadow in its yellow light
oddly at peace with itself.
My body, an ancient form, bends
through distance where something was lost,
a swirl of depth there
when I reach down, my hand
meeting with its darker brother
and a silent accord burns.
Here, in this dim hollow,
beaten, grounded, face to face with
the blank acceptance,
faceless expressions and
thankless intentions
I may never again see the light
that briefly shone between us
or the treasure of its purpose.

MVP 1933

I remember youth, glory, invincibility,
all that,
I was 13
on that day-
my friends weren't around
and my father wasn't at the bar
or even drunk
and he came down to the grass
to throw the ball with me.
Nothing extraordinary-
short throws only
but hard tight spirals.
He played for six minutes.
Threw the ball 27 times.
I remember the next day he took
his stiff arm to the bar
and I paced
football in hand.
Days came.
Weeks went-
and I remember that grass,
that most beautiful green grass
where I finally laid down,
still waiting.

Santa Cruz

Quaint crooked streets,
bookstores, cafés
and lights up and down a vesper beach.
Homeless hippies with cell phones
but confused at crosswalks—contemplating bridges.
Flip-flops, backpacks, beads, brims
beneath Blue Mountains of yesterday's lumberjacks.
Broadside faces of street musicians and masters
of Zen—celebrating defeat.
And I walk up to Water Street
turn right, cross the river
pass the cold stone silence
of the Santa Cruz courthouse
making for the motel-
I could almost love California again
so far behind me
now.
Hungry miners dipping pans
into cold discoveries of loss.

Dreamers in the Hands of Circumstance

Selling history by the chapter
hindsight by the year
doleful in approach
hopeful in retreat
words
rolled from parched lips
cracking with exhaustion that need
confirmation of the second
The sealed sacrifice
of an ordinary life
dying by the second-
Nobody knows the beat of the heart
Nobody knows the flight of the bird
Nobody knows the substance of a single second
as the trust
the sacrament
the love
the fields
burn away

Awkward Sun

Awkward sun
Breaking clouds
Yesterday's snow scattered
on hillsides
The bluebird leans
infinite
in autumn chill
Distant mountains shrouded
not by storm
but by warmth
of change never-ending
So difficult
from lives like ours
to see the difference
as we slowly erode
year by year

On the Eve of Enchantment

It is not by season
or circumstance
nor sorrow or elation
that brings me closer to your world
Not by heated anger
or frozen hindsight or
words spoken softer
than the petals of an Easter lilly
Not by a certain forgiveness
or danger of demise or
cheers and heckling
of those watching-

I return because I never left
I'm here to claim my heart
in a place to call home
to receive unto myself by giving
myself back
To ride the midnight horse
into the bloom of light
which needs no title
or reason for being

River Oak

Naked
Bent by survival
Clutching empty air
as if to savor memories
that came and went
with an October breeze
only to be caught
unguarded by seasons
all along the river
leaning towards one another
waiting for the first bud
to try again

Even the Clouds

Darkest hours circle 'round
weakest moments
Even clouds have stopped-
silent wings of a magpie
overhead ripples
of distant mountain range
lean and wait. If
your world crashes in
look outward. If
your soul reaches out
look inward. If
you've given up
close your eyes
and wait-

What Else Do We Know

Another year abandoned
to hindsight
Everything is in retrospect
of the human eye
What else do we know?
In the woods
just beyond the tree line
the nocturnal gaze in upon us
Do they wonder why we hurry?
Do they wonder why we wait?
And over
a cold winter valley
a perfect V formation of geese flies
People look up
trying to judge time.

Claw

It comes for you
in precarious hours
between shades of darkness
smiling like a sinister child
It is a movement in your skull
It is a prayer in a closet

It does not hate you
but seeks you out
like a bloodhound on the trail
lumbering through blackened woods
It is a meddling finger
It is a clawing of light
It is a touch of warmth

And you turn away

The Greatest Poem

The world will never see the world's greatest poem
because it was screamed from the blood-caked lips
of a Fourth Street prostitute bent
over the police hood as the nightstick came down
Or muttered mundanely from a warehouseman
dreaming of the light of day
Or whispered subconsciously by a bus driver in Jerusalem or
an Iraqi child looking at something in the sky
It was cursed by a soldier looking for his foot
and a parcel delivery man in Cleveland
as the breaks locked up
It was prayed by an atheist in a subway fire
and by newlyweds in a Tel Aviv nightclub
when a man entered wearing a heavy coat
in August
It came through laughter
It came through tears
It has been spoken
but not heard

The world will never read the world's greatest poem
because it was never written but it was felt
by a paraplegic and a million mothers
of molested children
It was a needle prick for a man in a Philadelphia alley
and a child's embrace for a blind woman in Seattle
It was a dream to some, a dream
which no language has words for
And it was a place, a place too high
and a place too low for our boundaries to recognize

and it is day
and it is night
It is you
It is me
and these things just can't be written

and the clouds circle
as the tombstones crumble
and the wind blows on through the pass
and the world will never see the world's greatest poem

Kamikaze Soup

I cling to your absence
It's all I have left
At sun-up you pour me
a hot cup of illusion
I drink it in morning
I drink it at night
I drink the moisture from your lips
your neck
your thighs
I drink the moisture of your disappearance
and choke on the dry ash
of a winter dream
I cling to your silence, wrap limbs
'round abandonment

I cling to the sterile scribbling pen
of the Doctor
It's the noise of my life
He gives me a prescription of isolation
I drink it in morning
I drink it at night
The room is large, airy, metallic
Angry walls echo silence
I breathe it in
A picture of an Orchid above
and my palms grow moist
clinging to stillness
form muted words
around a flower of deadness

I cling to gentle midnight blindness
It is all that I see
Black dawn pools before me
I drink it in morning
I drink it at night
before I open my eyes and know
you're not there
A blue shaft of light
where you know longer sleep
I breathe in the silence of your voice
moisture of breath
I cling to dry petals
Blue and muted
and I cling to a windowsill
spider web
I cling to distant barbecue smoke
I cling to a smile at the gas station
I cling to a child in sunlight
I cling to warm winter thoughts
and a cold summer chill
I cling to a ten hour shift and ankles
swollen and blue
I cling to thin air around you
I cling to the liquid of my passing
I drink it in morning
I drink it at night
I cling to everything that is
and everything that isn't

which is never enough

Redneck Jewish Deli in the Desert

by Scott Shulim

21st of Sivan

Since I can't seem to remember the date of your death
on my English calendar,
I circle the date on my Jewish calendar:

the 21st of Sivan.

That's the date my mother, our mother
has been reminding me of every year at this time,
for every year that has passed since you passed.
14 years, 14 consecutive reminders from my mother
   (our mother, mom).

I'm 39 now. Mom is 75. Dad is 83. You would have been 42.
   Assuming everyone has their day to die, assuming our parents
   don't die at the same time, our mother will remember to remind
   me of the date you and our father died. Or our father will remind
   me of the date you and our mother died. When they're both gone,
   nobody will be around to remind me of anything. Except you.
   Would you be so kind?

The 21st of Sivan. You'd think I'd remember it. You'd think I'd hang
   onto it for dear life.

A Bagel from My Homeland

I wake up hearing
the passionate smacking
of my great uncle's lips,
thick and moist from Poland
taking life from a freshly-baked bagel
with cream cheese and lox and raw onion

sucking the life out of the leavened
symbol of the flavor of
the sweat of generations of
Jewish bakers and bakers' wives,
like the wife of my great uncle,
my great aunt who used to swallow
my face with love
and feed it scrambled eggs
fluffier than every cloud
in the universe:

the secret in her fingerprints, the flavor in her veins.

I taste the eggs and smell the green
of Monticello spring and see
my great uncle's '63
great white shiny Chevy
and dream of using it as my winter fortress
to throw snowballs at the Irish kid with the dress.

"Look at you! You eat like a bird!"

I look up and see the wrinkled surface,
blink back tears of misplaced rage

and eat my eggs real fast
not like a bird
because I'm scared of my great aunt
who's usually gobbling my face
but now looks ready to smack it.

Smack smack smack
go my great uncle's lips
on the freshly-baked bagel
with cream cheese and lox,
devouring the symbol of
the flavor of my homeland.

Another Day at the Office (Vague Entity)

I dreamt our office had been attacked by a tornado bomb. One
    industrious young woman
had been virtually sliced in half, her green oozing innards flowing out
    of her in viscous sheets. Rather than diminish in stature, she
    became bloated with importance, first her torso
and then her head, and she managed to plow through her To Do list
    as if there were no tomorrow.

Another co-worker, who shall go nameless, suffered a vicious stab
    wound to the back,
but still managed to coordinate a 12-way conference call after she
    died.

Our building had been infiltrated by a smallpox earthquake, but there
    were still deadlines to meet
and promises to keep. Plus I had a couple of errands to run at Rite-
    Aid.

Bingo, The Forgotten Sport

Septuagenarians
nodding in rhythm
sedated serpents.

"B 1."

Befuddled hearts
hope against hope
for something
to hope for.

"I 32."

Filmy eyes widen
to take in
their last chance
of happiness
since
someone shouted

"N 56!"

Empty chair
at table 47.
Somebody died.

"G 78."

A man sits up straight.
He's 83 1/2.
He's awake and alert.
Dad?

Bitter Fish

Chew but don't taste
taste but don't swallow.

Swallow then regurgitate bitter fish.
I'm tasting bitter fish and memories
washing down my windshield,
reflecting twilight yearnings for recent histories
I'm reconstructing.

Blood-Soaked Mambo

Fire shoots up
in rhythms older than
fire escapes
and ancient agreements
among boys

in a place
where you don't react to the glint of a knife
with the sharpness of your intellect,
where dance is a rite of passage
not just rapid, lively movement.

Bulletproof Flag

I am a Sikh American. I drive a bulletproof cab with flags and slogans that shield me. Allah is not enough. I am an American of Sikh heritage. I love mankind and will not harm you. Please do not harm me for whom I resemble. There is only one God I believe in, and he is devoid of hate. Your nasty stare is reflected in my headlights. Please turn it off.

Chaste

Let's say you pretend you've never done anything like this before.

Say something like, "My lips have only brushed my dreams."

I'll pretend I'm the ambassador of shame, bearing gilded gifts of guilt.

Then, I'll ruin you without even touching you.

Comic Book

Parked outside the comic book store in the rain
coated with traffic
he can't stop remembering,
his feet slogged in syrup
waiting for her spirit to come back
on the next plane.

Her emotions were cartoons
all kerplunk kerblang kapoww.

Couple On the Beach

"When they buried your sister,
they buried your laughter," he said.

He was thick with scholarly stylings.
She was lying under a different sun.

Depressive

Plans to make,
bed to make,
make you stay.

Time to mourn,
life to mourn,
mourn to live.

All the weight
of the world
on my neck.

None of the strength of Atlas.

Drowning In Stages

I.

The first wave of grief
comes in with the tide
of tears I can't
differentiate
from saltwater
or urine.

The second wave
washes with the tears
of a candle
waxing poetically
over a bread dish
on a wooden table
from Ethan Allen.

The third wave
tastes like the tear
of a baby
crying out
for the heat
of its mother.

II.

Where does the wind
blow
when it's lonely?
Through my ears,
through her legs
unaware?

Does she shiver from the cold
or the memory of the boy
who once passed
between her
and what once passed for
ecstasy?

Why is the wind
cold
when I'm lonely?

III.

The tips of my fingers
are numb
turning blue.
I don't know how to feed them.
I should have let
the feeling
feed my fingers
and not
let my fingers
feed my greed.

I want to taste the tears
of a baby crying out
for the heat of its mother.

A Most Embarrassing Moment

I wish I were a (renegade) beagle,
putting the area where my balls used to be
on display for dinner guests.

Instead, I am just a man letting out
a 10-second creaking-door fart
during a lull in a client meeting.

Empire

This far up you can see ten years back:

you've got a radio show
a Columbian girlfriend
the world is yours.

North

Columbia School of Journalism is waiting,
questioning your lack of ambition

South

God plays the Brooklyn Bridge like a harp
so high

so high
you can measure its span with thumb and forefinger.

A man with a squeegee
sits beneath the muddy brick,
stuttering out his pain
and the love that rinsed away with the rain.

So high

so high
you can crush his dreams
with your thumb and forefinger.

Northeast

Another gilded art deco phallic-inspired spire
sways toward you as the lights come up.

The windows are eyes watching
a man getting his teeth cleaned
80 stories above the dirt,
his soul a gaping cavity
no drill will ever fill.
so close

so close
you can hear
your friend's youngest daughter breathing, "Mira, mira, McDonald's!"

A fast-food
free fall
down to earth.

Endings (Fear of Beginnings)

Endings (Fear of Beginnings) part I

If I stand still
it will come to me.

Not gradually
but suddenly
like a Mack truck death.

A fear
not of endings
but of beginnings,
of things
to start over.

I dread
the break-the-seal
unstuffed cotton
chemical whiff
new

of new friendships
circles
backroads
nightmares.

If I lie still
the fear will fill the darkness
under my bed.

A fear
of beginnings,
of things
to turn over.

I cower before
the shrink-my-head
unstuffed casket
formaldehyde whiff
new.

Endings (Fear of Beginnings) part II

If I shut up, I can hear the sounds of my family
yet-to-be.
The daydream is lily-white and well-to-do and idyllic.
A suburbia coma.

The location is Long Island, Sparks, Asheville, Woodstock, Grass
    Valley.
If I shut down, I can hear the laughs of metal lounge chairs splashing
    in the pool
and the screeching brother and sister mingling with the splashing
    brother and sister
to form one whole nostalgic note.

They're my unborn children and I love them even if they're not
    geniuses or budding triathletes.

But my outer fortress impenetrable defense ends the romance before
    it begins.

Endings (Fear of Beginnings) part III

If I stand still
it will come to me.

A fear
not of endings
but of beginnings,
of things
to start over.

And it won't come gradually
but suddenly
like the Mack truck death of my unborn child.

Endings (Fear of Beginnings) part IV

I grab hold of a much bigger hand
before I face
the first-day-of-school
unpacked notebook
Elmer's glue whiff
newness of everything
that takes me away
from the friends I've made.
That pulls me away
from the voices and faces
I know by heart.
The music and words
that pump my blood.

The things I do that allow me to say,
"I'm a writer."
to beautiful women at parties
without bashing my head through a wall.

So I'll do the difficult thing.
I'll meet new people
in another place
and care about them
like I think about us
and start again.

Endings (Fear of Beginnings) part V

"Are you feeling better?"

    "No."

"Are you feeling a little better?"

    "No. Are we landing yet?"

"Almost."

    "What's our plane look like?"

"I'll show you."

    "Where's Mommy?"

"She's not here anymore."

        "I knew that I knew that I knew that I knew
            that...I...just...ask...you...to...make...sure..."

Exorcism

"Mother? Make it stop!"

You cannot remove my voice
from the muttering leaves

my step from beneath
your floorboards

the ghost of my breath
from the back of your neck.

(It starts with) the smell of the rain
the rustle of a bedsheet
a push in the small of the back.

Even the boogieman's left me alone.
As alone as the lonely face in the moon.
I am the loneliest man in the room.

My skin is the surface of the moon.

No closer to being with you than being on the moon.

False Teeth

I found a pair of false teeth lying on the ground
in the false shimmering summer
of Baltimore's famed Harborplace
and feigned interest in them
under false pretenses.

I attempted to wonder whose mouth they belonged to,
and when they were separated from the make believe person's maw
as I posed as a man who cared about my fellow man.

Nobody believes me.

First Class

Board when you damn well please
we'll float you on a wider cracker
practice looking smug, looking
floating in a wider wrapper
give us your power suit
we'll stick it on a wider hanger
apocalyptic visions
encapsulated in a wider paper
tally ban new cue ler tax cut snooze
pour my coffee through a wider filter
first class pilot lift the nose
control your member with a wider lever
trouble again with engine four
kill it with a sweeping gesture.

First class body hits wider ocean.
Fold me in a wider coffin.

Fitting

"Everything okay in there?"

"I don't fit in here.
I'm too cheap for this raw silk.

The hem and drape are perfect,
but I am far from it.

And I cannot change my color and shape
with the seasons
without excruciating pain and mental anguish.

I don't fit in here,
and my stain will not go away
with repeated washings."

"Okay, great."

God Is In the Eyes

God is in the eyes
of a child
luminous and quiet as a prayer
for the dead,
longing to be connected
to the religion
of a lost soul.

And God is in the flakes of dried stadium mustard
in the corners of my son's mouth
late in the season for me
still early for him
still counting
the balls and strikes
of his heroes.

Godzilla Bomb

Stinky lunch boxes of nuclear waste,
fairy pants and asthma coughs
bigger than life.
Run! Run! Run for your lives!
It's the sound of squeaking brakes amplified to a horrifying degree
and the music couldn't be any worse!
Run! Run! Run for your lives!
Or the young flesh will bubble off your bones
and you'll die awake,
the terrifyingly bad orchestral music stomping your brain.
Run!
The double-headed bloated babies are coming to Kung-Fu your
    lunch box.

I Left My Heart In A Box In San Francisco

It needs exercise,
especially during the holidays.
Not enough air within these four gray walls.
It may be mistaken for a fruitcake
or a bomb.

It needs exercise
to catch the Christmas sun like memorabilia
to hang onto the longing of short-winded cable car
strangers it will never know.

It's a good heart
a crusty red bridge of a heart showing its age
a tower pointing to a group of has-been poets who won't turn the
    page.

It needs exercise,
long steady walks up Telegraph Avenue
to withstand the bone-jarring, joint-cramping nights
inhaling the peeling stories told by the paint
in the Ocean Park Motel

the songs sung by the coffee mug
rings on the warped wooden floor
of a haunted studio space
with a very long hall
on the corner of Geary and 25th.

I left my heart in a box in San Francisco
pumped up in a locker at the airport

beating to the rhythm
of a new Chinese year.

It needs exercise
affection,
to be tugged by someone
it will never see again.

Home/Pacific

Home

He visits the old neighborhood,
feels himself pulled down
to the basement
to the laundry room
past the adolescent urinating
through his mother's apron,
and sees his conscience leak
from cardiac patients being mugged.

He visits the old neighborhood
and sings a song for the big garbagemen
sucked into the walls, the ceiling core, asbestos, vapor, sofa dust, raised
    bumps of gilt-edged caramel candy dishes,
    wall-to-wall carpet fur balls.

Pacific

No beach, no guitar, no blondes
no sun

just the bluffs to keep him company
and send him to sleep with his sister's words:

"Pull me out of the Pacific
save my soul from all the oceans
I'm alive, I'm alive, I'm alive."

I Read You

like the mammoth tome on the history of highways I promised to
return to my father after I was finished with it, but put off so long
that he died of boredom waiting for my enthusiastic feedback,
tired of waiting for my lazy vagueness to miraculously hone itself
into a sharply pointed ambition I could turn on anyone who was
in my way and accomplish the great things he kept insisting I was
capable of until he died.

Know Before Whom Thou Standeth

Young cantorial soloist
casts her spell upon
row after row of twice-a-year
brothers and sisters—

    (marry me quietly, liltingly)

Ancient Hebraic strains
shed their millenniums
to warm generations of dead
cold, irreverent hearts—

    (through soft, translucent lips)

Still, these ancient letters
stand only for ancient letters.

And though I worship the way
you stand and sing—

    (those are childbearing hips)

it's with a soul divorced from God's.

Little Italy

Until you've been inside the mouth of a mustachioed Italian woman,
  you'll never know the joy of the feeling of Spumoni melting on her
  tongue outside on the front stoop, sweating her brains out because
  her mustachioed husband bounced the air conditioner off the fire
  escape banister.

Metro

On the world's most towering escalator,
I will reach new heights of apathy.
I will drift into a coma on the way up,
and celebrate my past lives on the way down.

Parenthetical Family

two little girls

(not mine)

come bounding across the lawn

(my friend's)

with a handful of affection
and an ample if limited supply of dimpled, rosy cheeks.

They're so happy to see me,
their temporary friend.
The man who steals the funny page
till daddy's back on center stage.

Their breath smells like freshly laundered snuggles,
and their tickles and giggles
make me forget what day it is.

Till I remember.
I'm just a guest here.

My Friend's New Girlfriend's Sister's 31st Birthday Party (Salsa Night)

Forgotten tomorrows whispered coyly through a greasy serviette
a cowbell stick affectionately snatched from a drunken grasp
a weary hopeful impression on the arm of a loveseat.

Taking "If gringo here knew how to dance, he'd be up all night" as a
compliment.

I pass on the Courvoisier. It gives me nothing more than a little gas
and a little sadness.

Since the Last Time I Saw You

I've diminished.
News flows through me and I retain only the chunky remains of lesser
meaning; I'm a sieve.

I've accomplished nothing.
Nothing is expected of me, so I effortlessly achieve slightly more
which amounts to zero; I'm a machine.

I've acquired no courage.
I sit and stir until I hear the inevitable shocking news of the sudden
death of someone closest to me; I'm a cowardly seer with no vision.

Suicide Mule

The tourist turns to inhale the West,
scratches a patch of three-day-old ruggedness,
and dreams of treasures, movies, and exotic accents.

The mule lifts its tearful eyes,
turns to snort at the West,
and embarks on an endless trail of thoughts
and memories of kicking and spitting and pushing and shoving,
its body soaked with the fearful scent of urine.

It throws down the burdens of a generation,
takes a lumbering start,
and leaps into the Grand Canyon
to its next, perhaps easier life.

Terror

I fear alone.
I fear the pizza-provoked nightmare
before sleep.

I fear together.
I fear the paralysis-prone karma
of new beginnings.

I fear the panicky warmth
of collapsing tunnels.

I fear afraid.
I fear dread.

I fear dire warnings in general
and cold judgments in particular.
I fear the day of judgment.

I fear forever the empty sounds of self-satisfaction.

I fear physical authority
and I fear mental atrophy.

I fear catastrophic illness
and the stench of stillness.

I fear the nightmare that portends tomorrow,
and tomorrow.

The Drive Home

I can hear a stray leaf fluttering
around the engine bay.
A clock ticking
in a farmhouse on the horizon.
A worker ant panting
under the weight of a blade of grass.

I refuse to play the radio
or hear what's on your mind.

We could care less.

I might just fall asleep behind the wheel
so you can tell me how you feel
in the next world.

The Gathering (The Writing)

The harvesting of the poems, the polishing of the turds, the caretaking
of the pathetic, and the scrutinizing of the minutia.

It's time.

The sharing of the memories that are personal only to me.
The creating of the scenarios that are realizable only in the dreams
of a psychotic.
The preening for the adulation and the pining for the love
of a vacuous non-entity.

The writing of the sentences that begin with "the."

It has only just begun. And it has already ended.

The Gathering (The Reading)

I've been missing Monday nights
so uninspired
so tired
so mired
in sweet n' sour public confessions,
self-conscious mental masturbations,
and self-righteous mutual admirations.

You came for the sweat, tears, and libido.
I came for the mochachino.

The Gathering (The Mourning)

We sit and stare
at a stray (pulled) hair,
a young girl's yellowing tooth in a decaying album,
a one-eyed doll in a soiled dress sitting on the edge of a bookcase
swinging its decomposing feet.

Rapture slips from my grip
as flesh slips from the bone.

The mother wrings her hands and I nod unknowingly.
The family is strong enough to do what it is supposed to do
deeply whiffing the embalmed air,
comfortably nodding toward tradition,
but I'm uncomfortable with all of it:

being a source of solace
bearing canned soup and Entenmann's cake
keeping the dying chatter focused on the living spirit.

We slouch and stare
at the dense (harsh) glare,
no shelf to rest our eyes.
no place to vacate our thoughts.

Self-pity and apathy and all things ending in why
are inevitable.

Shall I hold your tear-soaked head in my lap?
Replace small talk with monstrous images?
Compare your loving daughter to a tamped out ember?
Quote Coleridge on the madness of death?

I prefer to speak of March madness
and the sadness of being beaten by a buzzer.

The Whole World Is A Poem

Propped up by other peoples' stories
not bits of journalist newspins of sketcher renderings of celebrity
    biographies
but full grown beings with pasts and futures,
    he screamed into a video poker machine,

"This whole place is a poem."

threatening to write one,
startling the underage deer caught in the headlights at the end of the
    bar.

"Why, the whole world is a poem."

> *The rivulets of tobacco juice leaking down Donnie Baseball's chin in
>   the fading light of home plate.*

> *The Harley freak financial planner rocketing west, an American flag
>   bandana over his mouth, an ejaculating train of thought
>   between his legs.*

> *The Rabbinical student stretching on her living room floor, inadver-
>   tently making the sign of the cross.*

"The whole world is a poem,"
he hollered.

"Shut up!
I can't hear the band!"
whispered the biker.

"You remember what you want to remember,
and leave the rest of us alone."

You, Me, The Wind, The Ice And The Snow

Your nails dig
into the palm of my hand,
the one that's not in control
as a diaphanous cloud of misunderstanding
is foreshadowed
by a chill,
a breeze,
a yearning
for a time
when we used to
rub together
like two nearsighted crickets.

My palm sweat sticks
in the crook of your elbow,
the one that once leaned on me
as a high pressure system of misapprehension
is forecasted
by a patch,
a swerve,
a burning
for a time
when we used to
blab together
like two shortsighted critics.

Our knees collide.

My car sneakers
begin to lose
their footing.

Chokehold

by Anthony Douglas Ziegler

When I Was Five I Played Games With God

I raced cars, pets, pedestrians, whatever
to lines on a sidewalk, street corner, fencepost,
or any other landmark I thought I could reach first.

I placed bets on my races
saying that If I were to win I'd live forever.

When I won
I raised my arms over my head
leaped, screaming for all to hear.

When I lost
I simply told God it was just a game
and walked away.

They'll Never Meet

She sleeps in a cloud.
It's the one she saw move over her
when she was in grade school.
Passing under sun clots in afternoon
back of her head in fresh cut grass
behind the playground
as the bell rang her tardy for class.

Tracing friends and family
rose closed eyelids
listening to her breath drag
its fingers over strings
heartbeat counting childhood
dying in shadows left by sun falling.

There is no epitaph
to be read out loud.
Just a rumor of what was once said
about her.
She could barely hear what they said.

Lawn mixed chamomile dust
rubbed the nape of her neck,
back of her thighs and forearms.
Fragrance of a musty textbook pillow
twists the nose and throat
as she listens for a bell
already missed.
It's a history book
she has little reason to read.

Why would she wish
to dig up the past?

 He walks to school by the mine
 where his father worked for years.
 It's a gold mine without the gold.
 Twenty years of pulling
 gold from rock
 and there is nothing left to remove.
 The veins in the rocks have collapsed.
 He turns his head enough to see
 the opening he had once watched
 his father move through
 like a final sip of red wine
 left spinning to the bottom
 spider-like webbing only enough
 to remember what color the wine was.

 The entrance is boarded closed.
 He'll have nowhere to work
 when he graduates
 if they don't find another place to dig.

History was never her strongest subject.
Sure, she learned of war
and the lives lost
or freedom found.
She tried to understand what
made war civil in the past.
She turned the pages
to the textbook under her other cheek
and read excerpts expected of her.
She took tests
wrote reports

and was graded on how well
she repeated what she'd read.

    He could've rode the bus to school.
    It would have picked him up in front
    of his house and he would have been
    on time, every day.

    Instead, he decided to walk alone.
    It was a long walk
    which allowed him to pass
    in front of the mine and be late
    for school, every day.

    He'd rather arrive late
    and see the mine doing nothing
    but sitting there in front of him
    wondering what might happen
    if he went inside.
    He wondered often about why
    they stopped pulling gold from the walls
    and when they decided to board it up
    and not return.

The track team runs around in the afternoon
kicking dirt in their tracks
hiding behind each other
trying to be the fastest in the world.
She sleeps with them running
around her, pretending
she doesn't exist.

147

Dreaming of Making Love

I keep your photos in Bukowski.
On the shelf in our living room.

When you go away
I awake exploring
pillow impression of your face
your body sculptured sheets
scent of hair.
I sit nude on the floor reading
thumbing through pages remembering,
looking past the ceiling
outside through our sky in syrup
left from pancakes eaten in bed
after early morning lovemaking.

I am you

where deaf walls absorb the glow of day
bleed a beat we've known as us,
awakened,

blues dropped, tilt head to taste the way smoke rises from the room
moves you over bent dirt roads
where I'll sleep under your head on my chest
your hands resting their strokes to join me.

I'd like to show you pictures of me
looking at pictures of you and me together
dreaming of making love.

Fat Chicken Popping

He died.
It's his fifteen minutes
and the best thing for him.

She still cries after six months
watching him thinning
not eating
trying to swallow air
saliva choking bugging eyes.

It's not over.
There is family within friendly thought.

We know our brother
by the fragrance our sister wears
to his funeral.

I'm watching the television like it's an egg
fat chicken popping out
on a Sunday morning.

The day after we buried him
we starve for forgiveness.

Management

He walked to work everyday for exercise.
It was an uphill path through citrus orchards bearing fruit year round.
The field workers threw dirt clods at him on occasion.
He stopped frequently to relieve himself.
Some trees grow taller than others.

"We cut their tops off to keep them uniform
and focused on producing fruit."

They were twenty long ass-kissing years.
One day he stopped working and became fat.
The hill no longer looked as steep.
The trees haven't grown in years.

I Cannot Remove Myself From You

News speaks in bullets flirting
"a 3 year-old was eating lunch with his mother at Burger King..."
you came in, three feet away
emptied your gun in his head
before he finished lunch
before he had a chance to finish life
before he had a chance to finish.

Who are you?

I have learned how to cry again
unplug the TV and pull the sheets over my face
after walking through my home
touching my children sleeping
with their stuffed animals
helicopters, rockets, airplanes hanging from the ceiling.

Who are you to decide
to wake up and load your gun?

I look in the mirror and see
"...blue eyes, brownish hair, 5'9", mid-thirties..."
They say it again and again.
I fit the description.

Who are you to decide
to wake up and unload your gun?

I cannot remove myself from you.

Photographs of a Woman on a Train in Canvas

Time to lay
down
pull the plug
on someone wanting
touch,
affection.

Strokes of oil
across canvas
waves on a beach.

Wet night
bonfire
tee-shirt
dancing
flat beer
showing nipples
without a twist of her hair.

This is a secret
only Victoria knows,
"I scream."

Teacher

In life
do we nurture our mistakes
to exaggerate the lessons learned?

Have we walked away
from our dreams to be focused
more intently on the emotions
of sound, sight, touch,
leading us as our means of understanding?

It is our song we hear.
It is what is played.

This song bleats boldly between buried words
while we watch
kicking dirt over our own faces
to ankles with toes still tapping
behind the voice of a teacher.

The Call

I exhale
chest falling or pushed in by pressures
from unknown or undefined or denied factors.

The phone rings.

My tea is too hot to sip.
The bagel listens calmly.

I hear it again
while my chest rises
around the dog, head twisting
looking over his shoulder
(do dogs have shoulders?)
at the phone as I trip on the rug
catch myself against the counter

The phone screams once more.
I answer, "Hello…"
Nothing moves
dog's tail stopped
attentive

you breathe my name.

Nevada is a Sleeping Orgy

I move myself through her
hair
fallen in piles of sand
and bush
hidden in speed
turning my affection to fairer parts of her body
I've not yet discovered
nor pressed my lip to cheek
to breast
or small of back.
I know her by compulsion
and the way she sleeps
body cresting round tips
of mountains
reminds me of finer fortune
found by lonely miners
touching one another in darkened evening rain.

Nevada is a sleeping orgy
with her valleys pure as cotton panties
lit like a Christmas tree on fire
and I move myself through her.

To Walk

We remember how to crawl
by turning.
There is something in a baby's first step.
No honed skill repeating.
Movement inherited perhaps
through courses of parental readings.

We walk to please a face
make smiles, clapping hands return us.
Photo opportunities end
the newness gone.

We run to arrive
or chase, escape.
We run.
A seemingly obvious progression from birth.
We run with finish lines in mind.
The goal, fruitful upon arrival.

All this learning to move has made us
weary and impatient.

It's where our feet are
which we find ourselves complete.
There is little in the way we move.
There is something in a baby's first step.

She Allows My Name (for Amy)

She allows lip quake to say
    my name
        as if pulling lemons from a tree.

Tight unbuttoned nipple
    tweaks eyes behind ice tea straw
        giggling drop spoon in sugar to crane.

Air changing mind mid flight
    returns to be heard. I bend
        wind through my ear.

She whispers it again,
    "Anthony"
        Gone.

Today. Passing childhood lemonade stands. Remembering.
    I say my name out loud
        beyond the scent of lemon.

Welcome Home

Can you feel me
behind the piano
playing hide-n-seek
with the babysitter.

It's very dark in between
where you've once looked
and where I'm attempting to be.

There is nothing in the air around us.

We find comfort in the hush of carpet
with stocking feet walking tiptoe,
peeking behind sofa
around bathroom door
under bed.

You pretend that I'm hard to find.

When you're tired
giving in to approach and have me
all at once with arms reaching
to squeeze, grab, swallow me whole,
I am gone.

I have left you standing without me.
There is no way to hold me tightly anymore.
How you remember me
is all I am.

Chokehold

You may soon forget to chase me down the hall
when the door swings closed
the new air pushes you to me.

Words Like That

I think of the moon
and the reflection it gave
through lakeside campfire
glowing water-colored nudes
playing drums stoned
in circles singing in rounds
eyes not full of self but seeing.

We are still singing.

You can hear our voices
like children watching ice cream
not yet melting down our cone.

There's a sky for words like that.

Ungrateful

I am ungrateful.

I look around watching them play.
That should be enough.

Nobody is earning any money.
There are necessities to keep our day moving,
to put us in a busy frame of mind,
which we may use to forget.
We may pass time not knowing.
This is a refreshing blessing.

I am aware
or perhaps not as aware as I may profess.
I worry where time may go
as it goes whether I take notice or not.
I would love the moment to stop,
look me in the face
while everyone I am apart of
may hold me all at once
so I may continue to breathe,
they may continue to play,
I may be grateful.

They're Asleep

Constant static surrounds a water ambush
internal spasms recalling
each limb reaching

scent of wood and ash
trees cautiously sifting cool air
squirrels scurry, jay screeches,
other birds share chatter
ricocheting off the valley
zippers like thoughtful raindrops
taking unpredictable turns
nylon crinkles and rests
occasional twigs snap on trails to the bathroom
pots and pans scrape over grills
hot water pops
coffee fights pine needle and dust of coals cracking
they draw themselves within their heads
pictures of how they'll look today
breaking eyelids open separately
come together to murmur standing apart
at distances not blocked
an impromptu choreography for a morning campsite
they're awake
the rivers still flow
and are barely heard

If I Could Say I Touched You

All night long
writing titles to poems that are
complete in themselves.

The Downfall of Literature and Poetry

She's been bitching
about the downfall of literature
and poetry
with today's youth.

She says,
"Short attention spans
are an obvious symptom
of youth."

I'm writing.
She has too much to say.
I'm twenty-five.

Two

Midnight
cerebral convention
with neon spanking school
teachers passing
chalk to a boy named David.

He wears no shoes
and speaks his own language
as if pulling the last feather
from a sleeping Indian's headdress.

The sum of two numbers
never makes him cry
when he is awake.

I Could

I could close these eyes
stop still within me
hiding my sight in my pocket lint
where nobody can see me.

There's a place I will remain
without thought
or image of your face
where I have no need to see.

I could shut my mouth
end words I breathe
restraining poetics in my cheeks
where nobody could hear me.

There's a place I will remain
without thought
or sound of your voice
where I have no need to speak.

I could.

I could.

Tapestry

In this walk
I've met sound, scent, hue
with no definitive boundaries,
mixing self with self
and me.

These exterior patterns are familiar
enough for me to lie down labels
draw arrows to their fragrance.

Their difference, I realize,
is not the shadow or shade
or even their placement in the world.
Their difference is within me.

My Death

I can imagine my death
like an empty milk carton
resting beside a bowl of rotting fruit
that she had no intention of eating
when she'd purchased it.

At First Glance

At first glance
the world is awakened
in needled breath, varied pulsing tones
knowing rhythmic chords
tweaking plasma pounding beat
toward every window curtain withdrawn
enough for eyes to dart through
and, if caught, offer a casual smile
insecurely with full tooth wide-eyed "hello"
before returning out of sight
and our returning to the next window glimpse.

At first glance
hands were bathed in circular lights
becoming aware of gravity, yanking cheeks
still bloody, mucus breathing
air exchanging vomit for sound
with motion gripping, tugging, pointing
with, at, to
all those shadows and shapes remain
not yet dignified with names
or roles they get to portray.

At first glance
there may be a friendly face
feeding me with her eyes holding me
touching and sharing my warmth
with others who mammoth both of us
dressed in pink and white stripped knee length
time softened cotton dress

freckled and giggling with my hand
arm shaking in her lap.

At first glance
I may see a reflection
with various colored wires
spaghetti swirling from bald head
eyes being interrupted, intentional diversions
brought by unpleasant shapes, unintentionally.

At first glance
there were seven of us
in a room I knew was white
beneath wallpaper crusted around breakfast nook
where beer bottles lined, ashtrays and pictures
of people and events I wasn't around
to be a part of.

At first glance
there was a light faced, cautious glimmer
moving toward me with half a fist shoved
backwards in her mouth
never blinking once
in a red velvet dress
nearly white hair parted down the center
blue ribbons with plastic poodles on them
and hands touching me like Christmas pudding.

At first glance
my bedroom was a closet
and my bed the second drawer in a dresser.

At first glance
I found the outdoors

Chokehold

to pull at my limbs and chest
vacuum lifting, separating eyes, toes
from fingers from face from sight.

At first glance
a red station wagon was
stuck in the snow on one occasion,
rolling freely downhill away from a garage sale
on another occasion blaming, shouting
early twenties parents
with the window closed, chasing.

At first glance
bearded man with belly sagging
pissing, drinking, smoking,
yelling to TV chatter
turns to see me from the open bathroom door
penis in his hand.

At first glance
a bottle of phenobarbital
dwarfed the dilantin by the kitchen sink
where my mouth watered.

At first glance
the tree in my backyard
could be seen from anywhere in Castroville
or the freeway returning home
pretending to sleep.

At first glance
a rock hit him in the face.

At first glance
the world is awake and breeds
in its own image, not fully recognizing
its reflection.

At first glance
there was a hand emphasizing
loud, full toothed, loose eyes darting
screeching, knuckle deep to cheek
gums bleeding beneath eyes swelling.

At first glance
there is an outline of beer cans
being huddled in plastic bags
shoved under a swinging bench
rusted and covered in red clay dust
everywhere except where he drank.

At first glance
she wore cotton panties
and tried to share them whenever she could.

At first glance
the oak leaves crunch under feet
softening to bleed and burn
between puddle jumping children
darting across dirt back roads.

At first glance
there was a picture of neighbors
on a fake fireplace mantel
left up for weeks after Christmas
because he hadn't come home.

Chokehold

At first glance
she seemed to breath with her eyes.

At first glance
they found him dead in an abandoned
three-story building where he'd been tied to a bed
at his request to help him kick heroin.

At first glance
the garbage disposal changes the way we look
at a fork.

At first glance
the seam of her pants was darker
even though the temperature in the living room
was around 69 degrees and falling.

At first glance
he disappeared around the corner
with a half dozen sheets chasing him
slowing behind and in their own sweat
until I'd thought he'd made it home safely.

At first glance
my 78 year-old neighbor
with the yard I wasn't allowed to cross into
died in his sleep while his wife
watered the lawn.

At first glance
I could fly if I tried hard enough
and believed I could.

At first glance
I remember seeing you somewhere, smiling.

At first glance
I could be everything to you.

Within Me

In solitude I find my reflection
in water rising
beneath the twist of a tree trunk
with arms extending to sky.

Inside pulsing fingers
caress this shell
with no dream time left
for conscious thought.

I dropped to knees already soiled.
No dirt here.
Just Earth and my touch
returning, knowing boundaries
so far from self
they are within me.

"Light. Air. Water. My Being.
…and all things I am rejoice."

Tomorrow

So, this is
what I'll think about
when I'm dead.

Words

Nothing creates love.
All is shared
in the words used.
It is awareness which reminds us
of the idea
to be loved
and to love.
The rest is motion.

0-595-28906-1

Printed in the United States
1319800004B/119